masaaki hatsumi
quintin chambers

stick fighting

techniques
of
self-defense

KODANSHA INTERNATIONAL
Tokyo•New York•London

Distributed in the United States by Kodansha America, Inc., 114 Fifth Avenue, New York, N.Y. 10011, and in the United Kingdom and continental Europe by Kodansha Europe Ltd., 95 Aldwych, London WC2B 4JF. Published by Kodansha International Ltd., 17-14 Otowa 1-chome, Bunkyo-ku, Tokyo 112, and Kodansha America, Inc. Copyright © 1971 by Kodansha International Ltd. All rights reserved. Printed in Japan.

LCC 79-158643
ISBN 0-87011-475-1
ISBN 4-7700-0963-1 (in Japan)

First edition, 1971
First paperback edition, 1981
95 96 15 14

Contents

Introduction

WE HAVE OFTEN wondered why the stick as a weapon has been so neglected in recent years. Inevitably, traditional forms of hand-to-hand combat were prejudiced by the increasing use of firearms, and yet, in spite of this, boxing, wrestling, fencing, and archery have all survived and even flourished in their sport forms. Until the early part of the nineteenth century in England, the art of the quarter-stave was an essential part of a man's education, and it continued to be practiced until very recently by the Boy Scouts. However, in general it is a forgotten art, and even among the police—the only people permitted by law to carry a stick as a weapon—the standard of technique is lamentably primitive.

Someone may well object, "Why should stick fighting be revived? Surely there are enough weapons already without reintroducing an art that has fallen into disuse?" The answer I think is simple. In every society there are people who resort to violence to cheat and molest innocent victims. If you became such a victim, you would have no wish to submit, and if you saw someone else being attacked, you would feel bound to go to his assistance.

If you are armed, of course, you will stand a much better chance. But which weapon would you choose? A gun is certainly effective, but it is lethally so. A knife is undoubtedly expedient, but if you use one, you are forced to kill or maim. On the other hand, let us not go to the other extreme and say of an armed assailant that he is merely psychologically disturbed and that we must avoid hurting him. Our aim, then, is to defend ourselves adequately, and at the same time to be able to control the degree of pain and injury that we inflict. Thus we must seek a weapon that, when used with skill, can overpower and subdue, without having such automatically lethal effects as a gun or knife.

Empty-handed self-defense has become very popular over the last few years. However, to be able to acquit yourself without injury when attacked by armed assailants requires a degree of skill that is achieved by few. A little knowledge is a dangerous thing, and this was never truer than in regard to fighting and self-defense. Yet it is astonishing to see how supremely and foolishly confident people can become after a few years' training in judo and karate.

All martial arts can be both creative and destructive. Used as a means of aggression, they will eventually destroy the person who thus misuses them. Used correctly, they can provide a stimulating and practical training, and at the same time they can be a means of education and discipline.

All these things we must bear in mind when we come to choose a weapon to defend ourselves with. It must be one that is incorporated into comprehensive technique with training exercises. It must allow us to disarm and control an assailant and, if the circumstances require it, to inflict pain on him, without running the risk of permanently injuring or killing him. In addition it is preferable that the weapon be commonly available or that objects similar to it are often at hand.

The stick fulfills all these requirements, and while in the West there are no fighting systems based on it still extant, in the Far East we find a comprehensive selection of techniques, for there the stick has held an honored place in fighting systems for many centuries. In fact, Japan's most famous swordsman, Miyamoto Musashi suffered his only defeat at the hands of Musō Gonnosuke, a master of the art of stick fighting.

The techniques described in this book, which might be described as a basic manual of self-defense stick fighting, belong to the *ryū*("system") called *Kukishin ryū*. Masaaki Hatsumi, the Master of the *ryū*, has adapted the techniques so that they may be of practical value today.

In Japan there are basically three types of fighting stick: the *bō* which is 5 feet 11 1/2 inches long and 1 1/16 inches in diameter, for which there are about 360 fighting styles; the *jō*, which is 4 feet 2 3/16 inches long and 7/8 inches in diameter, for which there are more than 70 fighting styles; and the *hanbō*, which is very often included among the *jō* and is 2 feet 11 3/4 inches long, or "walking-stick" length. The ways of using these three lengths of stick are of course different. This book is mainly concerned with how to fight with a stick of walking-stick length. Included here, however, are some techniques using a very short stick about one foot long. The origin of this weapon and the techniques that are suitable to its length is the *tessen*, a fan of which the outer sides and the folding leaves were made of iron. Since the techniques have been classified according to method of attack, you will find techniques of the very short stick interspersed arbitrarily throughout the book. This does not mean that that technique can only be used with that length of stick, since often either length can be employed. However, because leverage is important, *Tsuke iri* is very difficult with a stick much less than 15 inches in length, as is *Gyaku ude garami*. Similarly *Eda koppō* and *Hiki taoshi* become rather clumsy with the longer weapon.

We must think of a stick as anything that can be used as such, but it is extremely important to choose a technique to suit the weapon. If you try *Kyōkotsu kudaki* with an umbrella, all you will do is end up with a bent umbrella, whereas if you happen to be holding an umbrella any technique in which you can use the ends of it would be suitable. Pens, rulers, cigarette lighters, table cutlery, etc., are well suited to techniques like *Eda koppō*, *Uko arashi*, or *Nage kaeshi*. We must train ourselves to regard everything as a possible weapon and use our imagination to find techniques that are suitable.

It is not possible to include every eventuality, and it may be that in the course of practice you will find that your final position is different from that illustrated. This may mean that you have not followed the descriptions or the pictures carefully enough, or it may be due to the fact that people react differently. With some experience and experimentation you should have little difficulty in adapting your technique to meet the situation.

The authors wish to express their gratitude to Tetsuji Ishizuka for so uncomplainingly taking the part of the adversary, and to Atsuko Chambers for doing the sketches and for her invaluable assistance with problems of translation.

Fundamentals

There are numerous ways in which you can hold the stick; with it above your head, or behind your back, held in one hand or two, with one foot forward, and so on. The position shown overleaf has many advantages and unless otherwise stated is the one used throughout this book. In *Hira ichimonji no kamae* you stand holding the stick in both hands down in front of you. Your feet should be approximately 18 inches and your hands a shoulder-width apart. You must be relaxed and alert, but your aiertness must be an inner alertness which is not evident either in your stance or expression. From this position even if you are short of space to maneuver, you can easily block an attack. You can also thrust, strike, or push in any direction, and—most important—your elbows remain close to your sides and below shoulder level. Another important feature of this *kamae* ("stance") is that it is not an aggressive fighting stance. It looks perfectly harmless and can give offense to no one.

A weapon that is to be used in hand-to-hand combat must be felt to be an extension of one's own body and not a mere appendage. It follows, therefore, that correct body movement is essential to the successful execution of a technique. The most important movements to be studied are those that enable you to evade your adversary's attack. The eight basic movements are primarily evasive and only secondarily do they include retaliatory action. You would be well advised to practice them first of all without a stick to give yourself sufficient confidence in not relying upon a weapon for protection. These movements should be practiced many times until such proficiency is attained that your training partner can attack with full force and speed. These are exercises in timing and judgement of distance, and also in learning to strike correctly and to focus the weapon just short of the target. Although the more dangerous techniques of *Kukishin ryū* have been omitted there is still a very real element·of danger, and the greatest care must be taken during practice to avoid injury to your training partner. At the same time your practice must be realistic; in other words if your partner does not feel pain or feels he need not submit, you must continue to apply the technique until he does. It is a grave mistake for him to submit too soon or for you to apply the technique too weakly, for in this way neither will learn its true application and capabilities.

Hira ichimonji no kamae

SECTION 1
Basic Movements

BASIC MOVEMENT 1

Naname ushiro omote waki uchi

"Moving diagonally back outside his attack and striking the side"

Stand facing your training partner in *Hira ichimonji no kamae*. Start all the basic movements from this stance.

Your partner punches straight to your face with his right fist. Step to your left rear with your left foot and slide your right foot a little to your left, and at the same time swing the stick to strike him across the solar plexus. As you step with your left foot, your left hand must slide to the end of the stick, and as you swing the stick, your right hand must slide a little toward the left-hand end. This coordination of foot movement and hand

sliding applies to all the basic movements except No. 8. You should strike not so much with your hands and arms as with your whole body. After the completion of the movement, both you and your partner return to your original positions. He then attacks with the other fist. Whenever you strike you should try to make contact with the last 5 or 6 inches, where the maximum power is concentrated.

From Basic Movement 1 continue with *Tsuke iri*, Technique 1.

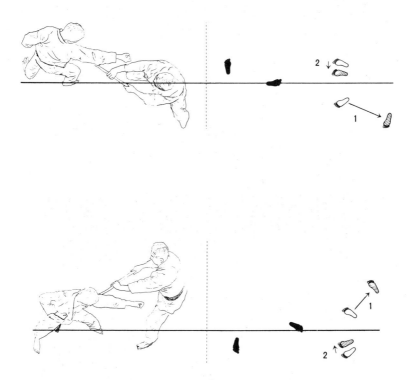

BASIC MOVEMENT 2

Naname mae ura waki uchi

"Moving diagonally forward inside his attack and striking the side"

Your partner punches straight to your face with his left fist.
Step to your left with your left foot and swing the stick to strike him across the ribs. Continue with *Koshi ori*, Technique 2.
When you are familiar with these two movements, practice them together. He attacks with his right fist, you step to your left and apply No. 1.
He attacks with his left fist, again you step to your left and apply No. 2.

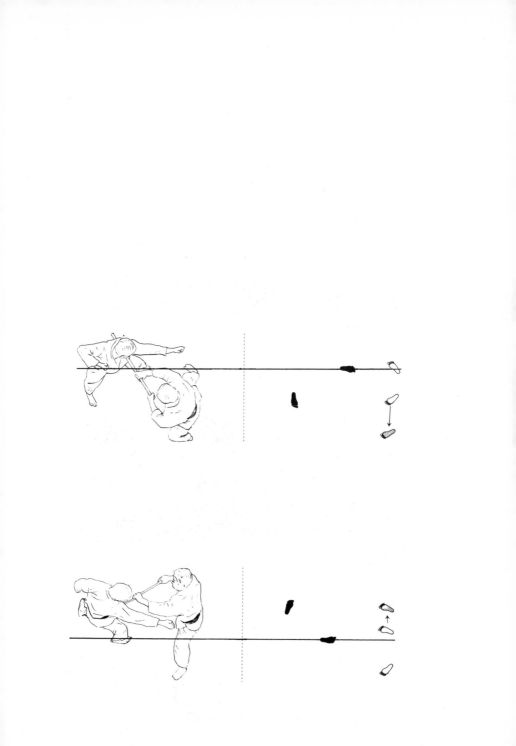

BASIC MOVEMENT 3

Naname mae omote waki uchi

"Moving diagonally forward outside his attack and striking the side"

Your partner punches straight to your face with his right fist.
Step to your left front with your left foot and slide your right foot in the
same direction and strike him across the ribs. Continue with *Kyōkotsu
kudaki*, Technique 6.

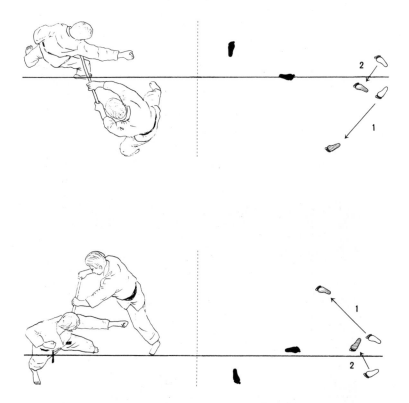

BASIC MOVEMENT 4

Mawashi kote uchi omote

"Rotate the stick and strike the wrist, outside his attack"

Your partner punches straight to your face with his right fist.
Step to your left or left rear with your left foot and slide your right foot a little in the same direction. At the same time move the right-hand end of the stick in a clockwise movement and strike down on his wrist. When he attacks with his left fist, the movement of the end of the stick will be anticlockwise. Continue with *Gyaku ude garami*, Technique 5.

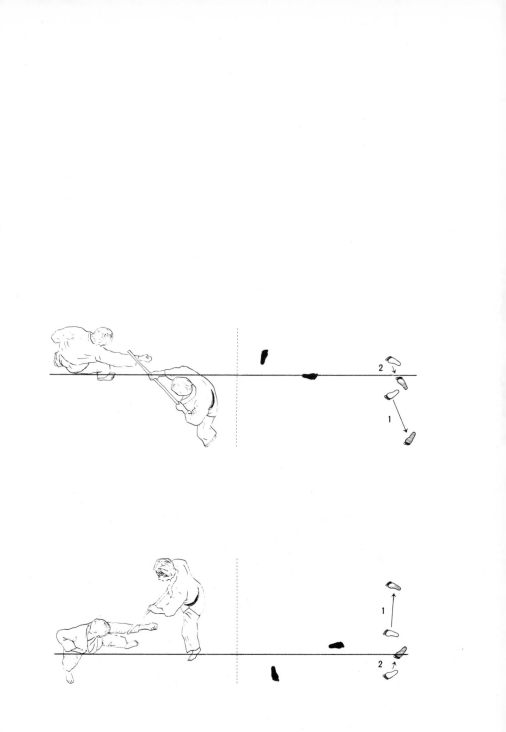

BASIC MOVEMENT 5

Mawashi kote uchi ura

"Rotate the stick and strike the wrist, inside his attack"

Your partner punches straight to your face with his left fist.
Step to your left rear with your left foot and move the right-hand end of the stick in a clockwise movement and strike down on his wrist. For a right fist attack the left-hand end of the stick must be moved anticlockwise. Continue with *Koshi ori*, Technique 2, or *Ganseki otoshi*, Technique 3.

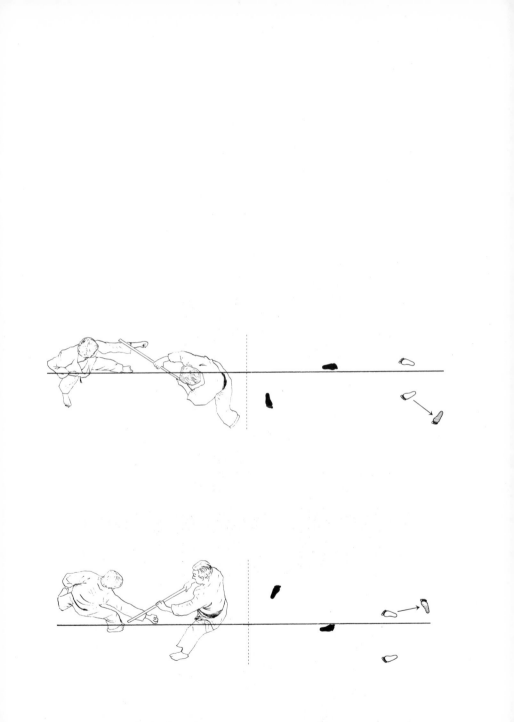

BASIC MOVEMENT 6 *Kote uchi omote*
"Strike the wrist, outside his attack"

Your partner punches straight to your face with his right fist.
Step to your left with your left foot and withdraw your right foot in an arc
to your left rear. Strike down with the left end of the stick onto his wrist.
Continue with *Ganseki otoshi garami*, Technique 3, Var. 2.

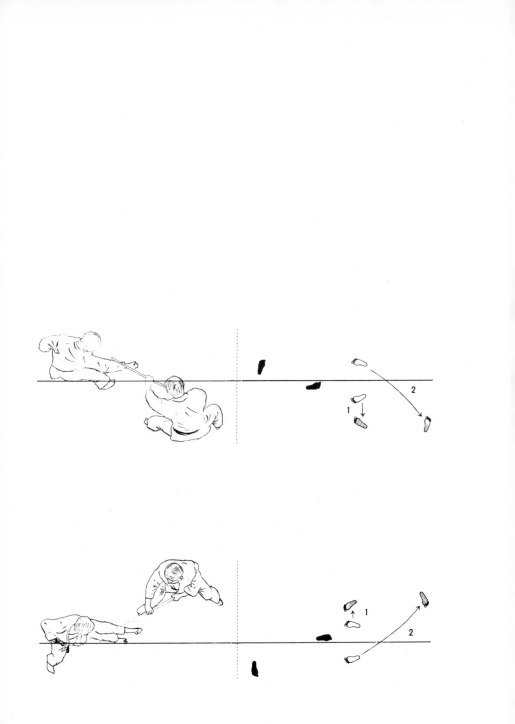

BASIC MOVEMENT 7 *Kote uchi ura*
"Strike the wrist, inside his attack"

Your partner punches straight to your face with his left fist.
Withdraw your right foot in an arc to your left rear at the same time pivoting a little on your left heel and strike down onto his wrist. Continue with *Ganseki otoshi*, Technique 3.

For further practice it is possible to work combinations of the basic movements, for example; your partner attacks with his right fist, you apply *Mawashi kote uchi ura*, Basic Movement 5. He immediately follows up with a left-fist attack, you withdraw your right foot and strike down on his left wrist with the left-hand end of the stick using *Kote uchi ura*, Basic Movement 7. He attacks again with his right fist, you withdraw your left

26

foot, sliding your left hand to the end of the stick, and strike down on his right wrist with the right-hand end of the stick, again using No. 7. He attacks again with his left fist, you use No. 5 striking down on his left wrist with the right-hand end of the stick. You will notice that the movements in which you come inside your adversary's attacking arm or in other words the *"Ura"* movements leave you vulnerable to a continuation of his attack. Consequently Basic Movements 2, 5, 7 and 8 should always be practiced with a combination in mind. This may be a combination of some of the Basic Movements or it may simply be a jab with the end of the stick to your adversary's face or ribs to better prepare the way for your application of a technique.

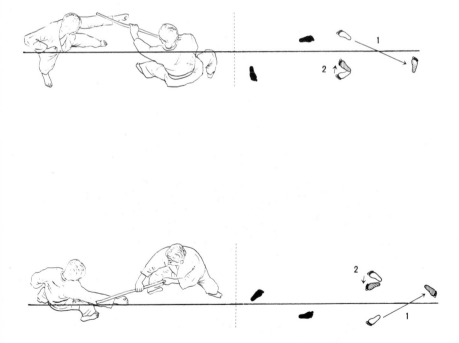

BASIC MOVEMENT 8 *Kata-te tsuki*
"One-hand thrust"

Your partner punches straight to your face with his left fist.
Release your right-hand hold on the stick. Step to your left front with your left foot and draw your right foot back a little, and thrust with the point of the stick to his chin or solar plexus.

An iron weapon suitable for the *Eda koppō* technique

SECTION 2
Techniques against Fist Attacks

Whether your adversary is attacking with his fists or with a weapon such as a knife or bottle, your response will be much the same. Your first purpose must be to disarm him by destroying the strength in his attacking arm. Do not be in too much of a hurry to apply a throwing or arm-entanglement action but defend yourself with one of the Basic Movements until a suitable opportunity presents itself.

TECHNIQUE 1

Tsuke iri

"Inserting the stick between arm and body"

▶ 1—2 Adversary attacks with his right fist. Step to your left and strike to his ribs or solar plexus as in Basic Movement 1.

3 Release your right-hand hold on the stick; grasp his right wrist and turn your left hand palm up.

Fig. 2 illustrates your striking against his ribs, but obviously if he is wearing heavy clothing you must choose a different target, such as his advanced leg or attacking arm. The choice of target must always depend on circumstances. You cannot be sure of the success of your technique unless you first inflict pain.

4 Straighten your left arm and putting pressure with the stick against his triceps force him to the ground.

5 *Immobilization* Keep your adversary's arm straight, palm down. Apply pressure to his triceps. You may also kneel on the stick between his arm and his body and on his wrist with your right knee to leave your hands free.

2 Koshi ori
"Breaking the hip"

3   Release your left-hand hold on the stick and grasp his right wrist. Bring the stick under his armpit, turn your right-hand palm up and extend that arm, stepping forward with your right foot.

2   Step to your right and strike to his ribs as in Basic Movement 2.

4   Thrust with your right hand towards a point behind your adversary's right foot, making sure that the stick does not slip from his hip. Apply pressure in this way with the stick against his biceps and force him to the ground. You may sweep his right leg from behind with your right leg to throw him with the judo throw Ōsoto gari.

▶ 1   Adversary attacks with his right fist.

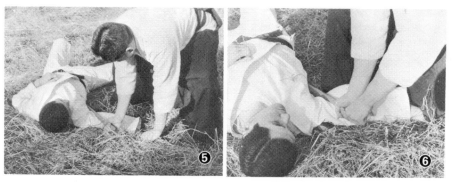

5–6 *Immobilization* Hold your adversary's arm straight. Apply pressure against his biceps. You may also kneel on his wrist and hold the stick with both hands or kneel on his wrist and on the stick to leave your hands free.

3

Ganseki otoshi
"Dropping a big rock"

3   Slide your right hand to the end of the stick, step forward with your left foot and strike to his ribs with the left-hand end of the stick.

▶1–2   Adversary attacks with his right fist.
Strike down on his wrist as in Basic Movement 7.

DISCUSSION———————————————————
In Fig. 5 and 6 your hips must be low, and there should be close contact between your back and hips and your adversary's front before you throw him.

4 Placing the stick firmly under his armpit, move your right foot behind your left.

5 Lower your hips and move your left foot deeply in front of him.

6–7 Twist your upper body to your right and throw him round your hip to your front.

3 VARIATION 1 *Ganseki otoshi makikomi*
"Dropping a big rock—enfolding technique"

▶1   If, while trying Technique 3, you do not enter deeply enough or if your adversary is experienced, he may be able to stay upright and resist your throw. In this case do not persist in this technique but immediately move into this variation.

2   Release your right-hand hold on the stick; thrust your open hand to his face; reach over his arm to take hold of the end of the stick and at the same time place your left hand close to his body. Pull with your right hand and apply pressure against his triceps. As he comes forward transfer your left hand to his wrist and force him to the ground.

DISCUSSION

Never let yourself be committed to the success of any one technique. From the position in Fig. 3 he may be able to roll forward and escape. If he does you can apply the immobilization of *Koshi ori*. You can prevent him from rolling forward by placing your right foot against his neck and shoulder.

3 *Immobilization* Hold his arm straight, palm down. Apply pressure with the stick against his triceps.

VARIATION 2 *Ganseki otoshi garami*
"Dropping a big rock—entangling technique"

▶1 This technique can be applied from Basic Movement 6 or if you are attempting *Ganseki otoshi* and he manages to slip his arm over your head.

2–3 Raise your right hand and pass the left-hand end of the stick over his arm in a circle to the front and bring the end under his upper arm.

DISCUSSION

From the position in Fig. 5 you can pull him to his right side or right rear in which case you can probably bring him to the ground with his arm behind his back and hold him in that position.

4–5   Trap his arm between the stick and your forearm. Move behind him and twist his arm behind his back; bear down with the stick against his shoulder.

6–7   If from Fig. 5 you push him forwards, he may manage to roll over and escape the arm entanglement. In this case bear down on his upper arm, and grasping his right hand press his wrist against the stick.

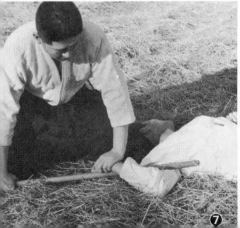

4

Oni kudaki
"Crushing the devil"

▶1 Adversary attacks with his right fist. Parry his attacking fist and grasp his wrist; strike with your fist against his upper arm (the inner side of the arm, the hollow between the biceps and triceps).

2 Pass the stick under his upper arm. Push his wrist towards his head with your left hand.

Alternative targets are:—
1a Adversary's biceps with the point of the stick. 1b His forehead with the end of the stick.

3 Bend his arm and pass the stick over his wrist; keep your thumb against his wrist but release your fingers to grasp the stick. Hold his wrist and the stick firmly together. Pull up with your right hand and push down with your left directly to his rear. If you push down with your left to your left rear you may dislocate his elbow.

4 *Immobilization* Pull up with your right hand, push down with your left; kneel on his elbow.

DISCUSSION

Fig. 2 shows your adversary with his arm straight; in point of fact, however, after your initial blow to his upper arm his reaction would be to bend it. If you have struck his forehead (Fig. 1b) and his arm remains straight, you can, after passing the stick under his arm and with it tilted towards you, bend his arm by striking sharply against the inner side or crook of his elbow, pulling down towards your waist. In the position of Fig. 3 you can either force him to walk or throw him to the ground.

4 *VARIATION* 1

▶1 Adversary attacks with his right fist. Step to your left and strike upwards at his elbow

2 Pass the stick under his upper arm and grasp his wrist.

3 Continue as in Technique 4.

4 *VARIATION* 2

▶1   Instead of holding his wrist and the stick together, you can pass your forearm over his wrist and under the stick.

2   Move your right hand round his elbow so that the stick lies across his neck. Thrust with your fingers toward his eyes to force his head back.

3   Reach your left hand behind his neck and grasp his collar. Pull down with your left hand and up with your right hand to throw him backwards.

4 *VARIATION* 3

▶ 1   Adversary attacks with his right fist.
Parry the blow with your forearm and strike his upper arm with the point of the stick.

2   Pass the right-hand end of the stick over his arm just above the elbow and pull towards yourself; at the same time push his hand back with your left hand and hook your wrist over the stick.

DISCUSSION

You will notice here that the leverage of the stick is very weak. This technique depends for it's success upon destroying the strength of his arm with your initial blow to his upper arm and upon its swift application. From the position in Fig. 2 you would be well advised, once you have bent his arm, to take hold of the stick with your left hand to release your right hand and pass it under his arm to take hold of the stick again, which will give you leverage on his arm. If his arm straightens with his palm towards you and his forearm against the left side of your neck, you can put pressure against his triceps, step back with your right foot and pull him to the ground. Refer also to *Yoko kujiki*, Technique 34.

3   Pull up with your right hand and push down with your left; go down on your right knee and hold his arm trapped against your waist and thigh.

5

Gyaku ude garami

"Entangling the reversed arm"

2–3   If your adversary reacts by bending his arm as shown, step round more to his right rear corner; move your right hand under his elbow so that the right-hand end of the stick passes under his upper arm and over his wrist. Move your left hand under your right to hold his wrist and the stick together. You may instead hold the stick only, with his forearm against the back of your wrist.

▶1   Adversary attacks with his right fist. Step to your left and strike upwards at his elbow.

4–5   Pull up with your left hand and push down with your right and turning to your right force him to the ground. When you have him in the position of Fig. 4, take hold of his clothing with your right hand as shown in 4a. This will give you better control of his movement.

6   *Immobilization*   Holding his wrist and the stick firmly together, apply pressure just above the elbow. You can turn his hand and press his ulna bone against the stick.

DISCUSSION

From the position in Fig. 2 you may hold his wrist and the stick together with your right hand and move your left hand to his rear so that that end of the stick is under his upper arm. Then push down to your right with your left hand. This method is easier to use but as you have your arms crossed it is not quite so strong. From the position in Fig. 4 you can release your right hand and take hold of the left-hand end of the stick, then release your left hand and pass it under his elbow to take hold of the right-hand end of the stick in the position of Fig. 7. You can now walk your captive forward under control.

3 Release your left-hand hold on the stick, punch him in the ribs with your right fist, and step round behind him. Your right-hand grip does not change; that end of the stick passes over your right forearm.

4–5 Take hold of the stick again under his left armpit.
Pull up towards yourself with both hands to put pressure against his chest. To immobilize him, drop down so that the stick is across his shins, pull back and topple him forwards. Withdraw the stick and place it across the back of his legs and push down. See also Technique 7, *Ryō-ashi dori*.

▶ 1—2   Adversary attacks with his right fist.
Step to your left front and sliding your right hand along the stick, strike him in the solar plexus or across the chest (Basic Movements 1 or 3).

7 Ryō-ashi dori
"Seizing both legs"

3–4   Move round to his rear and release your left-hand hold on the stick.
Pass it in front of his legs from his right
side.

5   Take hold of the stick again with
your left hand and pull straight back,
pulling his feet from under him.

6   *Immobilization*   Pressure with the
stick against adversary's legs.

2   Strike down on his attacking arm.

▶ 1   Adversary attacks with his left fist. Step to your right and raise the stick high.

DISCUSSION————————————————————————

In Fig. 4 instead of passing the stick in front of him at shin level, you may start at chest level and apply pressure against his ribs under his right armpit. See also *Taiboku taoshi*, Technique 46. As you go down apply pressure also against the outer side of his right leg, pull his legs together and push with your shoulder against the back of his thighs.

8

Kochō dori

"Catching a butterfly"

DISCUSSION

Notice that in Fig. 1 your adversary is preparing to follow up his initial attack with a right fist attack. As you enter in Fig. 2, either strike his face with your left fist or at least cover it with your open hand. Remember that an experienced fighter will always attack with a combination of fists or fist and foot. Indeed his initial attack may be no more than a feint, so you must be continually alert to change your tactics to meet the situation. From the position in Fig. 2, if you now raise your right elbow, you can trap his upper arm between the stick and your forearm. This gives you good control of his arm and you should have no difficulty in throwing him or walking him forward under control. After throwing him onto his face, keep your right-hand hold but slide your forearm under his and bend his elbow.

6 **Immobilization** Lean forward over him; pull up with your right hand and push down with your left; apply pressure to his throat.

4–5 If he manages to resist your movement, change direction, place your left leg behind his left; thrust the stick against his throat and, sweeping his leg, throw him to the ground.

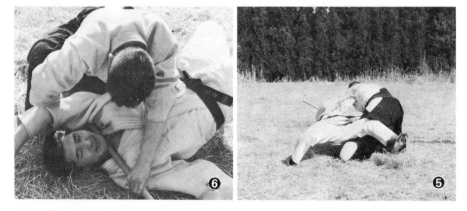

1 Adversary attacks with his left fist. Step to your left rear and with the movement swing the stick up to strike his upper arm or elbow; keep the little-finger edge of your hand uppermost.

2 Step in towards him; pass the end of the stick under his arm and tilt the end towards you; take hold of the stick with your left hand.

3 Put your left foot back close to your right, then move your right foot across in front of your adversary. Turn your body to your left and putting pressure against his upper arm bring him forward over your outstretched leg and force him to the ground.

9

Eda koppō
"Attacking the bones with a stick"

▶ 1   Adversary attacks with his left fist. Parry his blow with your left hand and grasp his wrist; slide your hand to cover his fingers including the thumb. At the same time move to his left side and thrust to his ribs below the armpit.

2   Keep a firm hold of his hand and hold the stick as shown.

DISCUSSION

From the positions shown in Figs. 3, 5, 6 and 7, you can control your captive and persuade him to walk forward, or you can force him to the ground and immobilize him. These two ways of holding the stick are full of possibilities. You should experiment against different parts of the body, both for striking and capturing. Pencils, bottles, cutlery, etc., also provide suitable weapons for this type of technique.

4   The stick may be held between the little finger and the ring finger as shown or between the ring and middle fingers.

3   Press the stick against the radius bone and hold the other side of his forearm with your thumb.

5   Hold the stick as shown in Fig. 4 and apply pressure against the lower side of the ulna.

6   Press the stick against the upper side of the ulna, just behind the prominent bone of the wrist.

7   Adversary's wrist captured between the stick, against the back of his wrist, and your thumbs pressed against the front of his wrist and palm.

10

Kata-te nage omote
"One-hand throw—outside"

3 Pull his right arm up and forwards in the direction of his right foot; at the same time turn to your left and place your left foot in front of his right and pointing in the same direction.

4 Step with your right foot to the right of his right foot and raise his arm above your head.

5 Swing his arm down in a circle to your front and with the movement step with your left leg well to your rear.

6–7 Twist his arm behind his back and grasp his fingers with your left hand.

▶1–2   Adversary attacks with his right fist. Hold the stick as in Technique 9 Fig. 4. As he attacks, strike down on his wrist and grasp it tightly. Press the stick against the lower side of the radius bone.

2a   You may also apply pressure against the upper side of the radius bone.

Immobilization (not illustrated)   When you have your adversary face down and with his arm twisted behind his back as in Fig. 8, you can hold him there by placing the stick across the back of his wrist and against his back; continue to bear down on his fingers with your left hand.

8   Use your right foot to assist you in bending his elbow. You can now release your right-hand hold on his wrist and use the stick against the back of his wrist or his elbow to bring him to the ground.

11

Kata-te nage ura
"One-hand throw—inside"

▶1 Adversary attacks with his right fist.
Hold the stick as in Technique 9 Fig. 4. As he attacks strike down on his wrist and grasp it tightly. Press the stick against the lower side of the radius bone.

2 Move his hand to your right and turn your body in that direction; turn your right foot.

3 Step with your left leg to a position in front of his left leg; bring his arm over your head.

4 Step well back with your right leg and swing his arm down in front of you.

5 Continue to twist his arm anticlockwise until he falls.

SECTION 3
Techniques against Foot Attacks

Defences against foot attacks do not lend themselves to such a variety of techniques as those against fist attacks or wrist holding for example. In the first place if you strike your adversary's leg as a preliminary to your technique, he will almost certainly withdraw it immediately, in which case it will be out of range for you to apply a technique against it. In the second place, as has just been mentioned, his fist may already be on the way and if you are not careful you may walk straight into it.

To be on the safe side it is advisable to be content with some form of striking action as shown on page 62 and continue with an appropriate technique taken from one of the other sections. Do not, however, neglect this section for though the techniques are difficult and require skillful body movement and good timing, a knowlege of them is important. Take, for example, the situation in which you have thrown your adversary to the ground but have not managed to immobilize him. He may be lying on his back with his feet towards you, kicking at you to prevent you approaching. In such a case it should be no problem to trap his leg in one of the ways shown in this section.

Striking Actions

● Step to one side and strike across his shin.

● Drop down well to one side and strike back-handed against the back of your adversary's platform leg. Aim anywhere below the knee.

● Holding the stick in both hands, block his kicking leg, either across the sole of his foot or his shin, depending on how he kicks.

12 *Ashi kujiki*
"Wrenching the leg"

▶1   Adversary attacks with his right foot.
As he kicks, step to your right and strike against the inner side of his knee or shin.

2   Pass the end of the stick under his thigh and step in towards him so that your left hand is against the inner side of his knee. At the same time you may thrust your right hand to his face.

3   Reach with your right hand over his thigh and take hold of the stick close to his leg; pull with your right hand to bend his knee.

4   Pull up with your left hand and push forward with your right and swivel the stick round his leg so that it presses against the inner side of his shinbone. Prevent his leg from turning by pressure with your left elbow against the outer side of his foot. Apply pressure against the inner side of his shinbone.

12 *VARIATION* 1

In this variation you attack your adversary's far leg or, if he is kicking, his platform leg.

▶1   Your adversary's right leg is advanced. Step to your right and sink down onto your right knee; strike backhanded against the inner side of his left knee or shin; thrust your left hand into his face.

2   Reach across his leg and take hold of the stick.

3   Push your right hand in the direction of his left foot so that the stick lies alongside his shin and your wrist against his foot. Twisting your body to your left, pull back with your left hand and push up with your right.

4   Push down with your right elbow to put pressure against the inner side of his shinbone.

13 *Ashi ori*
"Breaking the leg"

3 Bear down on his calf with your forearm, palm down, to force him to the ground. Pass the stick across his calf and take hold with your left hand.

2 Raise his leg onto your shoulder and, pushing against his calf, turn to your right so that he faces away from you.

4 *Immobilization* With his foot held in the crook of your arm, put pressure on his calf. If you cause him pain in this way, you should be able to transfer your attention to his upper body and effect an arm or wrist capture. See also *Benkei dori*, Technique 45.

▶ 1 Adversary attacks with his right foot.
Step to your right front and lower your body with your weight on your right foot; release your left-hand hold on the stick and catch his leg from underneath with your forearm; strike against the inner side of his left knee.

65

14

Ashi garami
"Entangling the leg"

▶1   Adversary attacks with his right foot.
Step to your left and catch his leg from underneath with the stick.

2   Release your left hand and pass your hand over his leg to grasp the end of the stick, palm towards you. Bend your wrists to hold his leg firmly in the triangle made by your wrists and the stick; push your elbows apart to scissor his leg and press with the stick against his calf.

15

Ashi dori
"Seizing the leg"

▶1 Adversary attacks with his right foot.
Step to your right and catch his leg from underneath with the stick. Trap his leg between the stick and your forearm.

2 Turning to your right, twist his leg so that he is facing away from you; thrust forward with your left hand in the direction that his left foot is pointing and throw him to the ground.

3 Thrust to the base of his spine or use the immobilization of Technique 7 to his right leg.

DISCUSSION

From the position in Fig. 1 you may pass your right hand over his leg and, taking hold of the stick again, capture his leg as in Technique 14.

TECHNIQUE **16** *Ashi gatame*
"Pressing on the leg"

3   Lower your hips and pass the stick
round the inner side of his leg.

▶ 1–2   Adversary attacks with his right
leg.
Step to your left and pass the left-hand
end of the stick under his leg from the
outside. His calf is now resting on your
forearm.

4–5 Move your right leg widely alongside your left so that you are facing your adversary squarely; at the same time the left-hand end of the stick will pass over his shinbone. In this way his leg is trapped between the stick and your forearm as in Fig. 5.

DISCUSSION

The position in Fig. 5 is in itself a painful and effective capture, but if you wish to reinforce it, you can pass your right hand beneath his leg and take hold of that end of the stick as in Fig. 6. You can now hook his left leg with your right and throw him backwards.

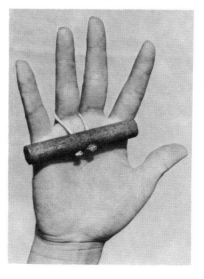

A wooden weapon suitable for the *Eda koppō* technique

SECTION 4
Techniques against Wrist Holding

The techniques in this section and those in other sections demonstrated with the short stick are not, historically speaking, those of the stick but of the *tessen*, or iron war fan, which was used in feudal times in Japan. Many of them can, however, be easily applied with a very short weapon or with a stick of walking-stick length. They should also be practiced with implements in daily use, such as pens, rulers, cutlery, etc. For their ease of application and great effectiveness and for the wide range of variations and combinations to which they are suited, they occupy an important place in the art of stick fighting. The imaginative exponent will no doubt discover many variations not described here and also combinations of these and the other techniques in this book. It is indeed hoped that he will do so since, for the arts of self-defense to be of practical value, they require the creative imagination of the individual. You will notice that the part of his wrist or foream against which you apply pressure with the stick will depend on how he grasps your wrist, whether from the top or from the side.

17

Ude garami
"Entangling the arm"

▶1 Adversary grasps your right wrist with his right hand.

2 Step forward with your right foot and lower your hips; thrust your elbow forward to put pressure against his thumb and thus bend his wrist so as to bring the stick across the back of his wrist.

DISCUSSION

It must again be emphasized that while applying these techniques you must put yourself out of range of your adversary's other fist, as in Fig. 7. Fig. 6 shows what will happen if you do not.

3 Pass your left hand under his wrist and take hold of the stick, palm towards you. Pull your elbows apart to scissor his wrist and apply pressure with the stick just above the prominent bone of the outer side of the wrist.

4–5 Step back with your left foot and pull down to force him to his knees. Do not pull so much with your arms as with your hips to bring him forward.

17 VARIATION 1 Ude garami omote
"Entangling the arm—outside"

 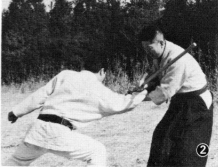

▶1 Adversary attacks with his right fist.
Move your upper body to your left as he strikes and parry the blow with your right forearm, catching his forearm between yours and the stick. Pass your left hand under his arm and take hold of the stick.

TECHNIQUE 18 Kasumi uchi
"Striking the temple"

▶1 Adversary grasps your right wrist with his left hand. Step forward with your left foot and back a little with your right and strike with the left-hand end of the stick to the side of his head.

2 Step back again with your left foot and bring the left-hand end of the stick up and back in a circular movement so that the right-hand end of the stick passes over his wrist from the inside.

3 Release your left hand and pass it under his wrist to take hold of the end of the stick, palm towards you.

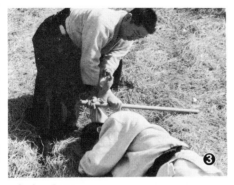

2–3   Scissor his arm in the way described above and pull him to the ground.

4   Scissor his wrist and pull him to the ground.

5   *Immobilization*   Kneel on his upper arm; grasp his hand as shown and bend his wrist. Press against the side of the spine to control his head.

19

Kyojitsu
"Feinting"

It is sometimes a desirable tactic in combat, as in any battle of wits, to deliberately show your enemy an apparent weakness in your defense, tempting him to attack you there. Another tactic is to attack, convincingly but not too strongly, so as to provoke a defense to which you have a counter. In Fig. 1 you have attacked in this way.

▶ 1   Your adversary lowers his body and seizes your wrist.

2   Pass the right-hand end of the stick over his wrist and across the back of his hand; pass your left hand under his wrist and take hold of the stick.

DISCUSSION

Notice in Fig. 1 that this is not the best way to strike at an enemy. A raised arm is easy to block and the whole of your body is exposed. If you should find yourself in this position, there are several things you can do. If the stick is long enough you may still be able to strike his head by turning your wrist. If you are armed with a truncheon you must first thrust your left hand to his face to prevent his right-fist attack, then push the truncheon through your hand so that it projects from the little-finger side of your hand. Then proceed with the technique as illustrated.

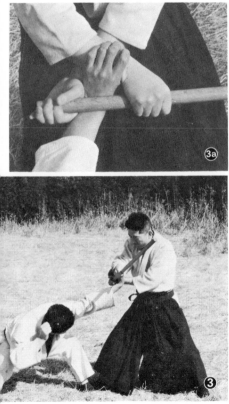

4 *Immobilization* Curl your wrists; push forward with your right forearm to bend his hand back.

3 Turning to your left push down with your right hand and, putting pressure against the back of his hand, bring him down in front of you.

20

Ude gaeshi
"Turning the arm over"

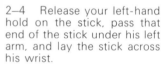

2–4 Release your left-hand hold on the stick, pass that end of the stick under his left arm, and lay the stick across his wrist.

▶1 Adversary grasps your right wrist with his left hand.
Step back with your right foot to put him off-balance in the direction of his left foot; strike with the left-hand end of the stick to the side of his head.

5 Take hold of the stick with your left hand and pull him onto his knees.

6 *Immobilization* Your adversary's hand is trapped between your right wrist and the stick and pressed against your right knee.

21

Take ori
"Breaking bamboo"

▶ 1 Adversary grasps your right wrist with his right hand. Turn your right-hand palm upwards until the stick lies across the little-finger edge of his hand.

2–3 Pass your left hand under his wrist and take hold of the stick, palm towards you. Scissor his hand, putting pressure against the little-finger edge. Pull him forward under control. Compare this with *Ude garami*, Technique 17.

DISCUSSION

If you are standing in *Hira no kamae* and your adversary grasps your left wrist with his right hand, you can apply a variation of the above technique. Release your right-hand hold on the stick and, turning your left wrist, let the stick fall across his wrist. Pass your right hand under his wrist and take hold of the stick, palm towards you. If necessary you can release your left-hand hold and strike him across the face.

22

Ryō-te dori
"Seizing both hands"

▶ 1   Adversary grasps both your wrists.

2   Release your left hand hold on the stick and move that hand towards your shoulder to break his grip. At the same time move your right hand across your body to your left beneath his right wrist.

3   Place the stick across his wrist, pass your left hand under his wrists and take hold of the stick.

4–5   Scissor his wrist; kick to his solar plexus or groin if necessary; step back with your right leg and pull him to the ground. See also *Ryō-te garami dori*, Technique 41.

23

Hon-gyaku jime
"Main reverse constriction"

3 Turn to your right putting pressure against the back of his hand.

2 Release your right-hand hold on the stick; take hold of the left-hand end of the stick with your right hand, palm towards you.

▶1 Adversary grasps both your wrists.

From the position in Fig. 1 you can release your right-hand hold on the stick and, stepping to your left, swing the stick across the inside of his advanced right leg. You will notice from this and the previous technique that it makes little difference whether he grasps one wrist or both; in fact it is probably to your advantage that he should seize both, since in this way both his hands are kept occupied.

4   As he turns his back to you pull straight down to his rear.

5   *Immobilization*   Either hold him with his hand trapped, or release your left hand and grasp his left wrist and strike his chest or appropriate target.

24

Kata-te jime
"Constricting one hand"

▶ 1 Adversary grasps your right wrist with his left-hand.

2 If you are holding the stick as shown in Fig. 1, you can of course apply Technique 20, *Ude gaeshi*, or you can step to your right and push the stick through your hand with your hip, so that it projects from the little-finger side of your hand.

4–5 Putting pressure against the back of his hand, turn to your left and raise your hands diagonally upwards so that he comes up onto his toes. In this position you can persuade your captive to walk forward. You must, however, keep his palm pointing forwards or straight up in the air, if you turn it further he will fall backwards as in Technique 23, *Hon-gyaku jime.*

3 Pass your left hand over his wrist and take hold of the stick, palm towards you.

25

Ude kujiki
"Wrenching the arm"

▶ 1 Adversary attacks with his right fist.
Step to your left and catch his wrist with your left hand; simultaneously thrust the stick to his face to strike or merely to distract him.

2 Step in close to his right side; catch his arm firmly under your armpit; at the same time pass the stick under his arm just above the elbow.

3 Take hold of the stick with your left hand and, turning to your right, bear down on his upper arm to force him to the ground.

TECHNIQUE **26** *Katame kujiki*
"Pressing and wrenching"

▶1   Adversary attacks with his right fist.
Step forward with your left foot and parry the
blow with the stick held vertically in your left
hand making contact just above his elbow.

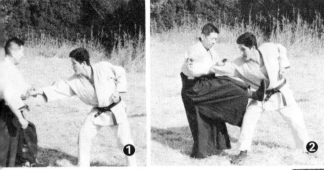

1–2   Catch his wrist in the crook of your arm
and take hold of the stick with your right hand.
If necessary, kick to his solar plexus.

3–4   Step your right foot to the ground and
bear down on his arm with the stick. If he keeps
his arm straight, put pressure against his upper
arm just above the elbow.

DISCUSSION

If in Fig. 3 he turns his hand palm up and
bends his arm, force him to bend it more
and apply a variation of Technique 4,
Oni kudaki. If he keeps his palm down,
bear down on his triceps just above the
elbow, pull him to his right front and onto
his face. Immobilize him by kneeling on
his wrist and leaning with the stick against
his triceps.

89

27

Tsure dori
"Arresting hold"

3   Slide your left hand under his upper arm so that the stick presses against his triceps.

4   Swing your right leg back and turn to your right; lift up against his upper arm with your left hand so that his elbow is twisted, and you will be able to walk forward with him held in this way.

2   Pass your right hand under his arm and take hold of the stick, palm towards you.

▶ 1   Adversary attacks with his right fist.
Step to his right side and parry the blow with the stick held vertically in your left-hand, making contact just above his elbow.

5   *Variation*   From the position in Fig. 1, keeping the stick pressed against his arm, swing your right leg back so that you and he are facing in the same direction. As you do this turn the palm of your left hand towards you and let the stick fall across his biceps. Pass your right hand, palm towards you, under his arm and take hold of the stick; scissor his upper arm and lift him onto your back.

28

Ude gatame, gyaku zeoi

"Pressing the arm, reverse shoulder throw"

3   Swing your right leg back so as to make close contact between your shoulder and his armpit.

4   Raise your left elbow and pull forward and down with both hands, sliding the stick down to his forearm, in this way putting strain on his elbow joint.

▶ 1 Step to your left as he attacks and parry the blow, making contact above the elbow with the stick lying over the top of his arm.

2 Step in with your left foot close to his right side; at the same time pass your left hand under his arm and take hold of the stick.

TECHNIQUE 29 *Ryūfū* "Dragon wind"

3 Pull his arm forward and step in close to his right side. Keep his palm up and make contact with the stick against his arm just above the elbow.

❷

2 As he brings his right hand forward, place the stick on your right shoulder and grasp his wrist.

▶ 1 Holding the stick in your left hand, strike your adversary's left arm. His reaction will probably be to hold his left arm with his right hand.

❶

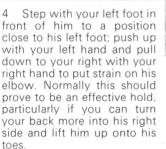

4 Step with your left foot in front of him to a position close to his left foot; push up with your left hand and pull down to your right with your right hand to put strain on his elbow. Normally this should prove to be an effective hold, particularly if you can turn your back more into his right side and lift him up onto his toes.

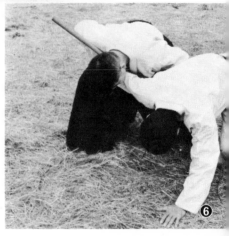

5–6 The only way open to him to release the pressure on his elbow is to push down on the left-hand end of the stick. If he should attempt this, thrust down with your left shoulder and pull down to your right hip with your right hand.

DISCUSSION

Needless to say, effective *Kuzushi* or breaking of your adversary's posture is essential in the stage between Figs. 2 and 3, in this case in the direction in which his right foot is pointing.

TECHNIQUE 30

Shibari koshi ori

"Tying up and breaking the hip"

This technique should be performed by two people, one on either side. Hold his wrist with his palm pointing forward. Pass the stick behind his upper arm and across his body, and try to thrust the end of the stick through his belt or into his trousers. Hold his wrist in place and push forward with your right hand to put strain on his elbow.

TECHNIQUE 31

Kote gaeshi

"Turning the wrist over"

▶ 1   You are standing in a right stance with the stick in your right hand. Adversary grasps your right wrist with his left hand.

2   Step with your right foot directly to your right; step forward with your left foot. Turn the palm of your right hand up and grasp his hand pressing your thumb against the back of his hand.

4–5 *Immobilization* Place your right knee on the ground close to his elbow and wrap his arm round it; turn your left hand in a clockwise direction, putting strain on his wrist and elbow. Prevent him from rolling over by pressing with the point of the stick against the back of his neck. If his right hand is within reach, you can lean over him and press the stick against the back of his hand (Fig. 5).

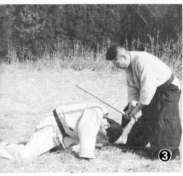

3 Twist his wrist and pull him down to his front, stepping back with your left foot.

2a Reinforce this with pressure of the stick against the back of his hand.

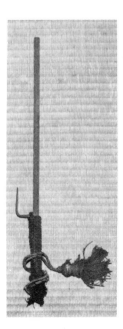

A *jutte*

SECTION 5
Techniques against Sleeve and Lapel Holding

When your adversary seizes your sleeve or lapel, you are in immediate danger since he now has considerable control over your movement, and this may be the prelude to a very swift attack. This attack may take several forms: he may merely wish to pull you forward or push you backwards; on the other hand he may attempt a throw, or butt you in the face with his head or bring his knee up into your groin. Your response must therefore be instantaneous. Ideally, by the time he has seized you, you should already have moved or at least prepared a move that will frustrate the coming attack.

32

Hiki otoshi
"Pulling down"

4 Take hold of his left hand with your left as shown here and in Fig. 7.

2–3 As he does this, thrust your left hand, palm open, to his face. Holding the stick with the long end against your forearm as in Fig. 1, press it against the lower side of his ulna bone and push to your left and roll his arm so that his wrist is bent and his body comes forward. Reinforce this movement with your left hand; step back with your left foot.

▶ 1 Adversary seizes your right sleeve with his left hand.

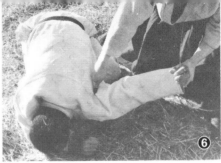

5 Turn to your left and turn his arm so that his hand is palm up. Press with the point of the stick into his shoulder joint and force him to the ground.

6 Immobilize in this position or hold the stick as in Technique No. 9 Fig. 4 and press it against his triceps.

4–7 Alternatively, from the position in Fig. 4, turn his hand away from you and press with the stick against his triceps just above the elbow and bear down on his arm and force him to the ground.

8–9 At this point, you may grasp his sleeve at the elbow, sweep his left foot with your right and throw him backwards to your right.

10 *Immobilization* Twist his hand away from you; push with your knee against the stick and bear down with the stick on his elbow.

33

Tsuki otoshi
"Striking down"

▶1 Adversary seizes your right lapel with his left hand. Strike the back of his hand with the point of the stick and press towards yourself. See Fig. 1a for detail. Step back with your left foot and turn your right side towards your adversary to put yourself out of range of his right fist. After using the point of the stick to strike the back of his hand, use the side of it pressed against his wrist or the back of his hand, reinforcing this pressure with your right fore-arm.

2–3 Step back further with your left foot and, leaning forward, force him to his knees.

34

Yoko kujiki
"Side wrenching"

▶1 Adversary seizes your left sleeve with his right hand.
As he does this, step back a little with your left foot and raise your left arm to make him believe that your attack is coming from that direction.

2 While he is distracted in this way, bring the stick over his arm above the elbow and take hold of the stick with your left hand.

DISCUSSION

After getting him off-balance as shown in Fig. 3 there are a number of other techniques you could move into. Technique 1, *Tsuke iri* is of course possible but more natural would be No. 3 Var. 1, *Ganseki otoshi makikomi*. If you press against the underside of his elbow, you can bend his arm and use Technique 5, *Gyaku ude garami*. Another effective measure is to pass your left hand over his upper arm and, taking hold of the stick, scissor his arm with the stick against his triceps.

3 Swing to your right putting pressure against his triceps just above the elbow. In this way force him to walk forward or bring him to the ground.

103

35

Hiki taoshi
"Pulling and throwing down"

▶ 1   Adversary seizes your left lapel with his right hand.
Grasp his right hand with your left; thrust the stick towards his eyes or against his cheek or under his chin to forestall a possible left-fist attack.

2–3   Strike with the point of the stick against the back of his shoulder joint and pull towards yourself.

4   Apply pressure with the side of the stick to his triceps and, pulling in the direction of his right foot, bring him to the ground.

5 *Immobilization* With your adversary lying on his face, kneel with your right knee on his right upper arm; reach over his body and pass the right-hand end of the stick, protruding from the little finger edge of your hand, under his upper arm.

6–7 Pull towards yourself and take hold of the end of the stick with your left hand; scissor his upper arm and pull towards yourself. Having securely scissored his arm you may now release the pressure of your right knee and, allowing your prisoner to stand up, walk him forward under control.

TECHNIQUE **36** *Uko arashi* "Attacking the neck"

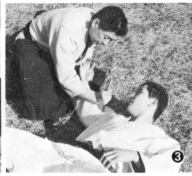

▶ 1 Adversary seizes your left lapel with his right hand. Grasp his right hand with your left, thumb against the back of his hand, fingers over his thumb and palm. Thrust the point of the stick under his chin to the side of his windpipe.

2 Step back with your left foot and turning to your left force him to the ground.

3 Strike his upper arm and push with the point of the stick into his face just below the cheek bone to immobilize him. This technique can also be used when you are unarmed by using your thumb instead of the stick.

37

Nage kaeshi
"Throwing down"

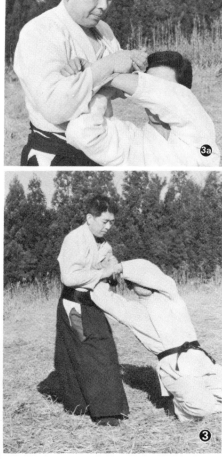

3   Twist him round so that his back is towards you and press the stick against the ulna bone of his left arm.

4   Step back with your right leg and push with your knee against his upper body. Immobilize him by trapping his wrists between the stick and your left thigh.

▶1 Adversary seizes your right sleeve and left lapel.
As he comes nearer to try a hip throw, shift your weight over your left foot, grasp his right hand with your left, and thrust your right hand forward.

2 As he comes even nearer and turns his body, thrust the point of the stick into his kidneys; at the same time push his right elbow to your right.

DISCUSSION

Whether you can bring this technique to the conclusion shown here will depend on his reaction to your initial preventive measure (Figs. 1 & 2). In any event you have ample opportunity to apply techniques to either arm.

38

Dō gaeshi
"Throw by pressure on the body"

▶ 1 Adversary seizes both lapels.

2   As he come near to try a hip throw, lower your hips and release your right hand.

3   Pass the stick across his chest, take hold of it again with your right hand and pull up sharply towards yourself. Jab your thumbs into his ribs.

4   Step back with either foot and pull your adversary onto his back.

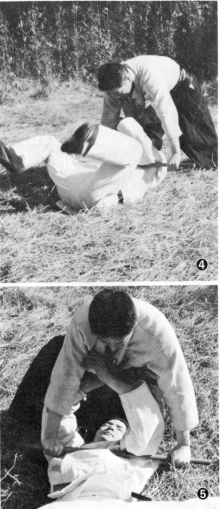

5   Immobilize with pressure against his chest. This can also be used as a conclusion to Technique 6, *Kyōkotsu kudaki*.

39

Gyaku zeoi
"Shoulder throw on reversed arm"

3–4   Grasp his left wrist and lift him up and forwards onto your back.

5   Throw him over your shoulder onto the ground.

6   *Immobilization*   Press the stick against his collarbone.

▶1 Adversary seizes both lapels.
You are holding the stick as shown in
Technique 9, *Eda koppō*, Fig. 4.

2 Strike upwards against his triceps;
step forward with your right foot.

DISCUSSION

From the position in Fig. 4, instead of throwing your adversary,
you can lift him onto your back and walk forward with him con-
trolled in this way.

TECHNIQUE **40** *Uchi taoshi*
"Pulling and throwing down"

If you are being attacked by several people at the same time, you may not have time to bring any under control, or if you are moving through a mob one of whom seizes your lapels it may be your purpose merely to break his grip.

▶ 1–2 As he attacks, raise the stick to strike smartly against his wrists to break his grip.

3–5   Strike directly forward against his breastbone and push towards his throat. Continue pushing until he falls backwards.

41

Ryō-te garami dori
"Seizing and entangling both hands"

▶ 1 Adversary seizes both lapels.

2 Release your left hand; pass your right hand under his wrists and place the thumb edge of your hand against his right wrist. Let the stick fall over his wrists; pass your left hand in front of your right and under his wrists to grasp the stick again, palm towards you.

3–4   Scissor both his wrists, step back with either foot and pull him to his knees. You can now raise him to his feet again and compel him to walk with you, or, by twisting to your left and pushing with your foot, turn him onto his side and hold him in this position. See also *Ryō-te dori*, Technique 22.

3   Release your left-hand grip and grasp his left wrist; pass the stick under his left arm with your right hand and lift sharply upwards and at the same time step to his left side.

4   Step with your right foot deeply in between his legs and force him to the ground with *Tsuke iri*, Technique 1.

▶1 Adversary seizes both lapels.

2 Step back with your right foot and lower your hips; pass your left hand under his right arm and thrust the point of the stick to his chin to put him off-balance and to break his hold on your lapels.

DISCUSSION

Fig. 2 illustrates one of the most effective defenses against this form of attack. If he attempts a stomach throw (the judo *Tomoe nage*), you can place the point of the stick in his solar plexus and thrust as he falls backwards. An alternative continuation from Fig. 2 would be to pass the left-hand end of the stick over his right wrist and, releasing your right hand, pass it beneath his wrist to take hold of the stick again. Scissor his wrist and pull him to the ground.

43

Ganseki dome
"Stopping a big rock"

3   Step with your right leg in front of his left;
pull forward with your right arm rolling his arm
so that it is kept straight with the palm down and
apply pressure on the elbow. From this position
you may strike at his left temple or flick the
stick across his eyes.

2   Pass your right arm under
his left, above the elbow.

▶ 1   Adversary seizes your collar with his left
hand from behind.
With the stick in your left hand strike back-
handed to his solar plexus to bring his upper
body forward. This is a dangerous blow with a
weapon of this kind so take care to use only
enough power to be effective. In this, as in all
striking methods with a weapon or without,
accuracy is infinitely more important than
power.

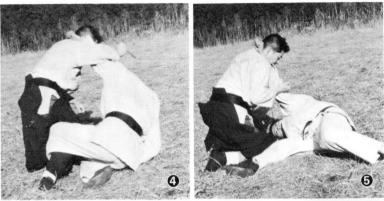

4   Turning to your left, throw your
adversary over your leg.

5–6   *Immobilization*   Take hold of the stick with
your left hand and pull towards yourself. With his
forearm against your neck, apply pressure against his
triceps just above the elbow. From here, there are a
number of techniques you can experiment with to
bring him to his feet and walk him forward under
control. See Techniques 9, 17, and 21, *Eda koppō*,
Ude garami, and *Take ori*.

A *jutte*

SECTION 6
Techniques against Seizure from Behind

To seize someone from behind with the purpose of holding him is not generally considered very good technique. For one thing there is not much you can do from that position, and for another you leave yourself open to several forms of attack. If, however, you should be attacked in this way you can: 1) stamp on his instep; 2) strike with your knuckles against the backs of his hands; 3) reach behind you and pinch the inside of his thighs; 4) arch your back, thrust back with your buttocks and at the same time butt him in the face with the back of your head; 5) lean forward and grab one of his feet as in Technique 45, *Benkei dori*. If you are attacked in this way it may be your adversary's intention to pick you up and throw you to the ground. To prevent this, hook your right leg round his right from the inside, then proceed with one of the escape methods of this section.

44

Ushiro dori tsuke iri
"Seizure from behind, attaching and entering"

2   Press the stick with both hands against his wrists to break his grip.

▶ 1   Adversary seizes you from behind.

3   Release your left-hand hold on the stick and grasp his left wrist.

4   Lower your hips and step with your left foot to your left rear; your right foot follows so that you are now on his left side. As you do this strike at his solar plexus with your elbow and raise his arm over your head

5   Bring his arm down in front of you and apply Technique 1, *Tsuke iri.*

45

Benkei dori
"Seizing the inside of the shinbone"

▶1 Adversary seizes you from behind.

2 The moment he seizes you, lower your hips stepping to your right rear; forcefully extend your arms to break his grip.

3 Bend forward and pass the stick behind his advanced leg.

4 Pull his leg forward to throw him onto his back. For extra leverage put your forearms on your thighs.

5 *Immobilization* No. 1 Apply pressure against his achilles tendon or calf; sit carefully on his knee. Since you have to keep tension in your legs to avoid causing severe injury to his knee, it is not possible to maintain this position for very long.

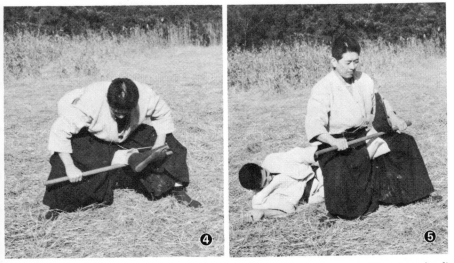

(see overleaf)

7–9 Turn to your right and step your right leg over his captured leg to a position close to his left knee.

6 *Immobilization* No. 2 Transfer the pressure of the stick to the outer side of his leg.

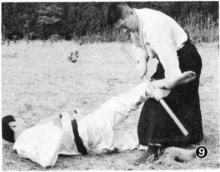

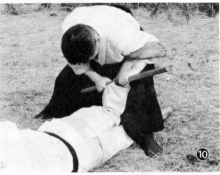

10 With his foot trapped in the crook of your arm, learn forward and apply pressure against his calf.

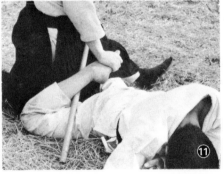

11 Grasp his foot with your right hand; turn to your left and go down onto your right knee. Lay the stick across the back of his thigh and across your own thigh; push with your right hand to put pressure against the inner side of his shinbone. See also *Sokkotsu ori*, Immobilization 4.

46

Taiboku taoshi
"Throwing down a big tree"

▶1   Adversary seizes you from behind. For this technique it is not essential to make him release his grip. Simultaneously thrust backwards with your buttocks and your head to make some gap between your body and his and extend your arms forward.

3   Take hold of the stick again with your right hand and pull hard towards yourself, putting pressure on his ribs.

2   Release your right-hand hold on the stick; lower your hips and step with your right foot back to a position behind his left, turning your body so that you are on his left side. Pass the stick under his right arm and across his ribs.

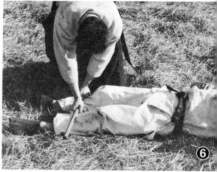

6 *Immobilization* Hold him with pressure against his shins.

4–5 Lower the stick to his knee level and pull towards yourself to throw him onto his back.

DISCUSSION

From the position in Fig. 3 you may strike against his hip as you lower the stick. In Fig. 5 if you pull back too strongly, he will fall with considerable force and may injure his head. If you bring your hands as close together as possible so as to bring his legs together, he will be much less stable, and you may ease him to the ground by pushing with your shoulder against his thighs. Do not, however, sacrifice safety to gentleness. Remember his hands are free to strike your head.

47

Tawara taoshi
"Throwing down a rice bale"

2   Holding the stick in one hand, pass it behind him and take hold of it again with the other hand.

▶1   Adversary seizes you from behind.

3   Arch your back and pull strongly, putting pressure against the small of his back. This should make him loosen his grip. Also snap your head back into his face.

4   Release your left-hand hold on the stick and continue with Technique 1, *Tsuke iri*, as in Technique 44, *Ushiro dori tsuke iri*.

SECTION 7
Techniques against Stick Holding

This section is concerned with those situations in which your adversary grasps your stick with the purpose of disarming you or attacking you with his other fist. The primary object of these techniques is to gain control of the stick and only secondarily to control your adversary, although in the process you will weaken his posture and should be able to apply an arresting technique. If you are attempting to disarm an adversary armed with a stick it might be good strategy to pretend to be interested in wresting the stick from his grasp but in fact apply some technique to his other arm.

48

Bō gaeshi
"Changing direction of the stick"

▶1 Adversary grasps the right-hand end of the stick with his left hand.

2 It is important in these techniques to use the leverage of the stick to nullify your adversary's strength. From the position in Fig. 1, try putting the stick into a vertical position simply by raising your right hand. You will find that he can resist you very easily. Now, without putting strength into your right hand, merely push down with your left hand using the leverage of the stick to arrive at the position of Fig. 2, at the same time step back with your left foot and lower your hips.

3 Push down with your right hand directing the point of the stick towards his belt; pull back with your left hand.

4 Slide your right hand along the stick to cover his fingers and press them against the stick. You may, of course, do this as soon as he grasps the stick. Continue to press down to bring him to his knees.

49

Kokū
"Empty space"

▶ 1 Adversary grasps the stick with his left hand to the right of your right hand and his right hand to the right of your left.
Step back with your left foot and lower your hips; push with your right hand to your left and with your left hand to your right so that the stick is vertical. At the same time cover the fingers of his right hand with your left and press his little finger against the stick with your thumb. You can also cover the fingers of his left hand as in the previous technique.

2 Pull back with your left hand and bear down with your right directing the point of the stick towards his right hip.

3 *Immobilization* With your adversary's right hand trapped, press down on his face with your right elbow.

DISCUSSION

Fig. 4 illustrates a variation supposing he grasps the stick with both hands inside yours.
The wider apart your adversary's hands are, the more difficult it is to apply this type of technique. In Fig. 1 you may have to change your right-hand grip and press with your index finger against his thumb. You can also force the little finger of his right hand sideways with your thumb and thus break his right-hand grip.

TECHNIQUE **50** *Awase nage*
"Meeting throw"

▶ 1   You are holding the stick as shown in this picture; your adversary grasps it in the same way.

2–3   With your adversary's right hand as the fulcrum of the movement, move your left hand up and forwards in a big circle to your front; simultaneously step forward and to your left.

4   Pull back with your left hand and push forward and down with your right to throw him onto his back.

50 *VARIATION* 1

A variation of the above is to change your hands so that your left is in front of your right. Again using his right hand as the fulcrum, push with your right hand towards his left rear corner so that his left hand crosses underneath his right. With him in this weakened posture, move your right hand down and back towards yourself and push the left-hand end of the stick over his left shoulder.

50 *VARIATION* 2

If your adversary is strong or if he has his hands wide apart, it will be to your advantage to widen your grip. In this variation move your right hand in between his hands and follow the same principle as described above. It will assist you if you cover his left thumb with your right and press the side of it against the stick.

TECHNIQUE 51

Tomoe gaeshi, ashi dori osae

"Throwing in a circle, seizing and pressing the leg"

▶1 Adversary grasps the stick and pushes you backwards.

2 You may fall backwards deliberately and apply this technique or it may happen that as he pushes you trip and fall.

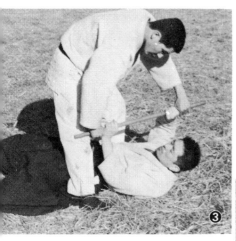

3   Strike with the left-hand end of the stick against his knee.

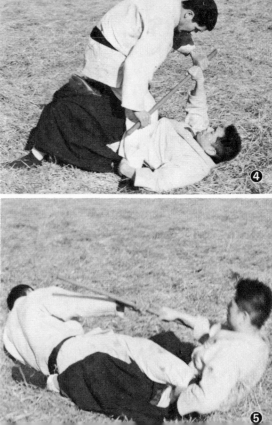

4   Raise your right leg and place your shin against his left inner thigh; take hold of his right ankle.

5   Push with your right leg and pull with your left hand and throw him backwards.

(see overleaf)

6–7 Strike with the right-hand end of the stick against his left knee or shin.

8–9 Raise your right hand and turn your wrist to break his grip on the stick, or, while keeping his foot tucked under your arm, use your left hand on the stick. An alternative is to cause him pain in his calf and thus force him to release his hold.

10 *Immobilization* Trap his leg under your arm and apply pressure against his shin.

SECTION 8
Immobilizations

IMMOBILIZATION 1 *Jō-wan ori*
"Breaking the upper arm"

You have thrown your adversary onto his face. Hold his wrist firmly against the ground; place the stick across his upper arm and kneel on it at a point between his arm and his body; press down on the stick with your right hand; slide your hand towards the end of the stick for maximum leverage. It makes little difference whether his hand is palm up or palm down.

IMMOBILIZATION 2 *Hiji ori*
"Breaking the elbow"

You have thrown your adversary onto his back. Hold his hand, palm up, firmly against the ground; place the stick beneath his arm at the elbow; kneel on his wrist and upper arm and pull up with your right hand.

IMMOBILIZATION 3 *Zen-wan ori*
"Breaking the forearm"

You have thrown your adversary onto his back. Hold his wrist with the thumb uppermost; press with the stick against the radius bone. Your right foot and shin should be placed against his side to prevent him rolling towards you. An alternative position is to place your right foot on the end of the stick closest to you and lean with your right hand on the other end.

IMMOBILIZATION 4 *Sokkotsu ori*
"Breaking the instep"

This could be used as an immobilization for *Ashi dori*, Technique 15.

1–2   Kneel on his right leg; pass the stick under his body with your left hand; with his left leg bent at the knee, grasp his foot and press the outer side of his ankle against the stick, pulling up with your left hand. A variation of this would be to force his left foot under the stick and push down with your left hand.

IMMOBILIZATION 5 *Ryō-te ori*
"Breaking both arms"

▶1   You have thrown your adversary with a technique such as *Koshi ori*.

2   Kneel with both knees on the stick.

3   Lean across his body and grasp his left wrist with your left hand; thread your right forearm under his upper arm and take hold of your own left wrist; pull towards yourself with your left hand and raise your right elbow (in judo, *Ude garami*), bear down with your left elbow on his face or throat.

IMMOBILIZATION 6 Ō-gyaku

"Big reverse lock"

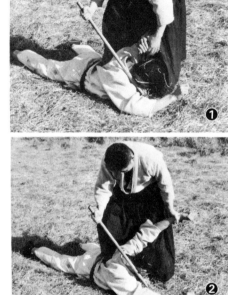

▶ 1 Having thrown your adversary onto his face in front of you, place your right foot on his back to prevent him rolling and place the stick against the right side of his neck, the point held firmly against the ground.

2–3 Extend his left arm and place his hand, palm towards you, against your waist. Press against his elbow to keep his arm straight.

4 Reach down with your left hand and grasp his right sleeve and pull his arm towards yourself; transfer your hold to his wrist.

5 Hold his wrist and the stick together.
In Figs. 1–2, you may find it preferable to get his left arm into position before placing the stick against the side of his neck.

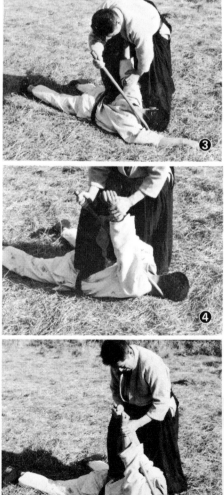

142

"Shaking and throwing down"

▶ 1   You have thrown your adversary onto his face; sit astride his back and press the stick against the back of his neck.

2–3   After inflicting sufficient pain to subdue him, quickly move his left arm over the end of the stick and take hold of the stick again. Pull up with your left hand to again put pressure on his neck. Lift his other arm over the stick in a similar manner.

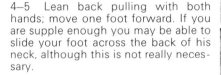

4–5   Lean back pulling with both hands; move one foot forward. If you are supple enough you may be able to slide your foot across the back of his neck, although this is not really necessary.

Glossary

Arashi: n. storm.
Ashi: n. leg.
Awase: n. from *awaseru*, to meet together.

Benkei: n. inside of the shinbone.
Bō: n. stick.
Boku: n. tree.

Dō: n. the trunk of the body.
Dome: n. from *tomeru*, to stop.
Dori or *tori:* n. from *toru*, to seize, catch.

Eda: n. branch.

Fū: n. wind.

Gaeshi or *kaeshi:* n. from *kaesu*, to turn over, throw.
Ganseki: n. a rock.
Garami: n. from *karamu*, to entangle, entwine.
Gari: n. from *karu*, to reap.
Gatame or *katame:* n. from *katameru*, to tighten.
Gyaku: adj. reverse.

Hiji: n. elbow.
Hiki: n. from *hiku*, to pull.
Hira: adj. flat.
Hon: adj. true, principal, main, regular.
Hō or *pō:* n. way, rule.

Ichimonji: the character for "one" in Japanese.
Iri: n. from *hairu*, to enter.

Jime or *shime:* n. from *shimeru*, to constrict, wring.
Jō-wan: n. upper arm.

Kaeshi or *gaeshi:* n. from *kaesu*, to turn over, throw.
Kamae: n. stance, posture.
Karamu: v. to entangle, entwine.
Kasumi: n. the temple (the side of the head).
Kata: num. adj. one.
Kataginu: n. stiff sleeveless robe for samurai on ceremonial occasions.
Katame or *gatame:* n. from *katameru*, to tighten.
Kochō: n. butterfly.
Kokū: n. empty space.
Koshi: n. hip, loin.
Kote: n. wrist.
Kotsu: n. bone. With a suffix beginning with 'h,' *kop;* eg. *koppō*.
Kudaki: n. from *kudaku*, to crush, smash, shatter.
Kujiki: n. from *kujiku*, to wrench, sprain.
Kuzushi: n. from *kuzusu*, to break; in Budō, breaking the adversary's balance.
Kyōkotsu: n. the sternum, breastbone.
Kyojitsu: n. falsehood and truth, i.e., deception, feinting.

Mae: adj. forward direction.
Makikomi: n. from *makikomu*, to enfold.
Mawashi: n. from *mawasu*, to rotate.

Nage: n. from *nageru*, to throw.
Naname: adj. diagonal direction.
No: possessive particle, of.

Ō: adj. big, great.
Omote: n. the outside.
Oni: n. devil.
Ori: n. from *oru*, to break.
Osae: n. from *osaeru*, to press down.
Ō-soto gari: n. major outer reaping throw.
Otoshi: n. from *otosu*, to drop.

Ryō: adj. both.
Ryū: n. dragon.
Ryū: n. style or tradition.

Seoi or *zeoi:* n. from *seou,* to carry on one's back.
Shibari: n. from *shibaru,* to tie.
Shimeru: v. to constrict, wring.
Shintō: n. concussion, shock, impact.
Sokkotsu: n. instep.
Soto: adj. outer.

Tai or *dai:* adj. big.
Taiboku: n. big tree.
Take: n. bamboo.
Taoshi: n. from *taosu,* to throw down.
Tawara: n. straw rice bale.
Te: n. hand.
Tomoe: n. huge comma, comma-patterned tile.
Tomoe nage: n. throwing in a big circle, stomach throw.
Tomeru: v. to stop.
Tori or *dori:* n. from *toru,* to seize, catch.
Tsuki otosu: v. to strike down.
Tsuki: n. from *tsuku,* to thrust.
Tsuke: n. from *tsukeru,* to attach, fix.
Tsure: n. from *tsureru,* to take along with one.

Uchi: n. from *utsu,* to strike.
Ude: n. arm.
Uko: n. anatomical term for the nerve at the side of the neck.
Ura: n. inside.
Ushiro: adj. rear, back, rear direction.

Yoko: adj. side.

Zen-wan: n. forearm.
Zeoi or *seoi:* n. from *seou,* to carry on one's back.